CW00704028

Skye
Island Beautiful

Skye

Jon Pear

Island Beautiful

DB PUBLISHING

To my wife Linda
Thank you

First published in Great Britain in 2010 by
The Derby Books Publishing Company Limited
3 The Parker Centre,
Derby, DE21 4SZ.

© **Jon Pear**, 2010

All Rights Reserved. No part of this publication may be
reproduced, stored in a retrieval system, or transmitted in
any form, or by any means, electronic, mechanical,
photocopying, recording or otherwise without the prior
permission in writing of the copyright holders, nor be
otherwise circulated in any form or binding or cover other
than in which it is published and without a similar
condition being imposed on the subsequent publisher.

A catalogue record for this book is available from the
British Library.

ISBN 978-1-85983-773-3

Printed and bound by Scotprint, Haddington, Scotland.

CONTENTS

ACKNOWLEDGEMENTS

Without the help and encouragement of the following people, this book would never have happened. Their patience in answering an endless stream of questions has illustrated beyond any doubt the kindness and generosity of the people of Skye.

Firstly, Cailean MacLean, who was instrumental in getting this book started. Then, in no set order of importance, Donald MacDonald, Graham Ross, Justin Grant, Robin Reid, John Holt, John Cameron, George Ingall, Myra McKinnon, Caroline MacLeod, David Shipman, Ken and Polly Bryan, Ian George MacDonald and Sine Gillespie. Special thanks also to Dan Corrigall and his two boat skippers, Ian and 'Squirell', whose boat-handling skills enabled me to get the images of the White-Tailed Sea Eagle. Lastly, I would like to thank everyone who has helped my wife Linda and I settle on this most beautiful of islands.

FOREWORD

From the time, more than five decades ago, when he was given his first camera, Jon Pear has been an enthusiastic and dedicated photographer. A camera upgrade, which saw him the proud owner of a Nikon F2AS, served to increase Jon's passion for the medium. He honed his skills at the Kingsway College in his native London, and over the years Jon has amassed a good deal of experience and an impressive array of accolades through his continued work in the photographic field. He ran a successful business in the south for many years, but despite this he had the very good sense to relocate to the Isle of Skye in 2004. At the risk of rehearsing the old cliché about London's loss being Skye's gain, it should be said that this island benefits hugely from people with skills and talent who come to live here.

As this impressive book of his photographs demonstrates, Jon has successfully reapplied the skills and experience he gained in London in an island setting. His work exudes a sensitivity of approach to subject matter, and Jon brings a freshness to the way in which familiar scenes are perceived and captured for posterity. There are many photographers who have attempted to record Skye's grandeur and, on the evidence of the photographs in this book, Jon Pear's work ranks among the most successful.

Cailean MacLean

INTRODUCTION

I first visited Skye 45 years ago when I was 13, with my brother and our parents. Even then, when a young teenage boy's interests lean towards the angst-ridden emotions of adolescence, I fell deeply in love with Scotland in general and the north-west Highlands in particular, with the Isle of Skye holding the favoured position as the crown among the visual jewels presented to me. Many more visits occurred over the intervening years, until finally my wife Linda and I found ourselves in the enviable position of having an empty nest. Our fledglings had flown and we were free to do as we pleased. It was only natural that we decided to up sticks and relocate to the Isle of Skye. Leaving behind children and grandchildren was not particularly easy, but we argued the point that they had, and would continue to have, lives of their own to live, and we owed it to ourselves to enjoy our middle age doing exactly what we wanted. So here we are.

From its volcanic past and beyond, Skye has been formed by a myriad of natural phenomena. Some of the oldest rocks in the world can be found in Sleat and these are estimated to be around 450 million years old and include Torridonian sandstone, Lewisian gneiss and other schists, shales, quartz and limestone. Mankind is estimated to have been here since the middle stone age (Mesolithic) period in around 6500BC. There are indications that these people changed from hunter-gatherers to farmers in around 3000BC.

Since then Skye has been populated by many different peoples: Celts, Gaels, Picts and the Norse tribes. Indeed, many place names on Skye are Nordic in their origin, while many more appear to have their origins in Gaelic or Celtic culture. From prehistoric times through successive settlements, the clan culture evolved and was dominated by the MacLeods and the MacDonalds. These two clans still have their respective headquarters on Skye today. 'Clan' means 'children' and 'mac' translates into 'of' or 'son of', so Clan MacLeod means 'children of Leod'.

Following the ignominious defeat of Bonnie Prince Charlie at Culloden in 1746, there followed a period of despicable mistreatment of the Highland and Island people by the government. Other sources can give more details of the atrocities committed by the government troops, but it was the banning of the tartan, the playing of the bagpipes and other traditional Highland practices that started the downfall of the clan system. Furthermore, clan chiefs sympathetic to the Jacobite cause had their lands confiscated. This led to the remaining clan chiefs increasingly aligning themselves with the government, and a more English style of landlord evolved. This ultimately led to the next unforgiveable sin perpetrated against the Highlanders – the 'Clearances'. The wholesale enforced removal of a people whose roots were firmly embedded in the Highlands involved some of the most brutal crimes against humanity witnessed in Britain. However, it must also be stated that the clearances involved many thousands of people leaving of their own accord to start new lives in the dominions. Many died on the passage due to the intense overcrowding, which meant that disease and illness spread rapidly through the ships. The population of the Highlands and islands has never recovered from this harsh regime of land management.

The census of 1821 shows that Skye had a population of 20,627. In 2001 the census showed the population to be 9,232, a 4 per cent increase over the 1991 census figures. Different sources give different estimates of the area of Skye; they range from 535 square miles to 639 square miles. Take your pick. Whatever the correct figure, the Isle of Skye is not densely populated, and both residents and visitors have a large area to enjoy some of the most spectacular scenery Scotland has to offer.

South Skye

The gateway to the Isle of Skye. Skye's controversial road bridge now offers faster access to the island, but has taken away the romantic aspect of 'Over the Sea to Skye'.

Kyleakin used to be the arrival point on Skye in the days of the ferry. This image shows the new community hall and in the far distance Castle Moil, which overlooks the harbour.

The traveller arriving from the direction of Plockton will be presented with a totally different view of the bridge. The lighthouse and cottages seen under the bridge are on Eilean Ban, a small island that was once home to Gavin Maxwell, author of *Ring of Bright Water*.

A charming open area for relaxation separates the cottages from the harbour itself.

Castle Moil still stands guard over the narrow seaway between Kyle of Lochalsh and Kyleakin. Formerly known as Dun Acainn (Hakon's Fort), in the late 15th century it was occupied by the Clan Mackinnon. Believed to be of Norse origin, its most infamous inhabitant was 'Saucy Mary' who, legend has it, ordered a chain to be stretched across the seaway to prevent boats passing without paying a tax.

Kyleakin is rightly famous for its population of otters *(Lutra Lutra)*. This sculpture, next to the harbour, is based on Gavin Maxwell's otter 'Teko'. It was generously donated by the creator Laurence Broderick.

Political decisions and falling prices have all but decimated Skye's fishing industry. Nevertheless, here we see a fishing boat returning to harbour to unload the day's catch, which is almost certainly shellfish.

A fishing vessel, now converted for use as a leisure craft, enters Kyleakin Harbour at dusk, watched by an inquisitive seal.

The old ferry slipway. Once very busy, it now lies virtually unused. It remains, however, an excellent place to catch a glimpse of an otter or two.

Kylerhea itself consists of a number of houses, many of which are holiday lets. No pubs or discos, but no shops or post office either!

The harbour is now mainly used by a variety of pleasure craft. The old tug in the background is not used and just lies quietly rusting away.

A small dinghy lies moored out of harm's way on the approach to Isle Ornsay.

Leitir Fura in Kinloch forest provides plenty of splendid walks with superb views to the mainland. This ruined crofthouse is part of a settlement abandoned in the early 1800s. It was left voluntarily due to extreme hardship.

Isle Ornsay lighthouse is actually on the islet of Eilean Sionnach. David Stevenson built the lighthouse, which came into use in 1857. In the mid–1960s Gavin Maxwell bought the lighthouse cottages along with those on Eilean Ban.

Sabhal Mor Ostaig is the only Gaelic College in the world. Opened in 1973, the new extension pictured here is situated amid breathtaking scenery. It provides a perfect environment for studying creative and cultural subjects.

Knock Castle lies on the coast of the Sleat (pronounced Slate) Peninsula and was once the stronghold of the MacDonald clan. Now in ruins, much of the stonework was used to erect local buildings.

The sea and coastal views down the Sound of Sleat are beautiful in all types of weather. This photograph was taken in May and shows the sun trying to break through the passing storm clouds.

The road down to Armadale is at its best around the month of May when the road is lined with a profusion of wild Rhododendrons.

The gardens at Armadale Castle are always a delight to wander around.

The paddle steamer *Waverley* is the last operational Clyde steamer and makes periodic visits to Scottish waters. Here she can be seen collecting passengers from Armadale Pier for short sea trip.

This photograph was taken from the stern of a private yacht as a service tender prepared to come alongside to collect a departing passenger.

This church near Sasaig enjoys wonderful peace and quiet, and again a profusion of wild Rhododendrons.

This lichen-covered rock faces out across Lochs Eishort and Slapin to Blaven (Bla Bheinn) and the Black Cuillin.

As you cross the Sleat Peninsula near the college, the hill above Loch Dhughgaill provides wonderful views across to the Cuillin.

Small secluded areas of Silver Birch trees can be found on the northern coastline of Sleat.

A fine day for grass mowing.

Byres, or outbuildings like this one, provide a welcome splash of colour with their rust–covered roofs. Often, though, the roofs have been painted red.

Tarskavaig enjoys the warm spring sunshine. In 2008 and 2009 Skye enjoyed some beautiful warm weather in April and June.

The island of Rhum on a warm, hazy afternoon.

The ruined church of Cill Chriosd (Christ's Church) lies on the B8083 from Broadford to Elgol. The graveyard has headstones which date from recent years back to mediaeval times. This church dates from around the 16th century and was built to replace a far older building, parts of which can still be seen on the west gable.

An early morning at Loch Cill Chriosd. This reed-filled loch was at one time haunted by an evil spirit, which St Columba is believed to have chased away in AD 570. Today it is a firm favourite with photographers.

In a few short moments the light can change and Blaven (Bla Bheinn) becomes ominous and threatening.

Early on a winter's morning Blaven is a delight when viewed from Camas Malag.

An old boat near Elgol.

Elgol seen from the south–west.

Dusk at Elgol. Rhum is on the left of the picture and Soay on the right.

A rainbow over Sgurr Na Stri, Elgol.

A fine view across Loch Scavaig to the Black Cuillin.

Detail from a burn near Torrin.

Rock formations on the shoreline just south of Elgol harbour.

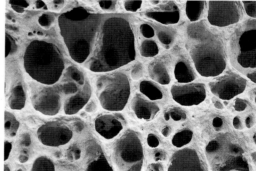

The honeycombed rock on the Elgol shoreline dates from the middle Jurassic period. The mixture of quartz and calcium carbonate in these rocks can lead to some unique patterns due to weathering.

Broadford Bay at 6.30am, all calm and serene.

Broadford and Beinn na Caillich, photographed from near Waterloo Point.

Unique patterns are formed in the grazing areas of the shore near Breakish.

The Red Cuillin Hills, photographed at dusk from Breakish, south of Broadford.

Snow covers Beinn Dearg
Mhor at the inland end of
Loch Ainort.

Central Skye

A traditional blackhouse, now serving as a very popular holiday let.

A house on the Island of Scalpay, viewed across Loch na Cairidh at Dunan.

Golfers on the course at Sconser.

View from Sconser golf course towards Ben Lee.

The Old Bridge at Sligachan with part of Glamaig in the background.

HMCC *Seeker* patrols the Sound of Raasay.

Eas a' Bhradain (Waterfall) on the long climb over Druim na Cleochd (Ridge of the Cloaks).

Sligachan Hotel lies at the landward end of Loch Sligachan and is an extremely popular starting point for a number of hill walks.

The Red Cuillin at dusk.

Glamaig in a cloak of snow and cloud.

Sgurr nan Gillean and Sgurr am Basteir reflected in a lochan on a fine spring day.

Marsco late in the afternoon on a winter's day.

A similar shot taken late afternoon in mid-autumn.

A slightly different view taken from Glen Drynoch.

The road into Glenbrittle.

A view from near the top of the Fairy Pools back towards Glenbrittle.

A view from the Fairy Pools, Glenbrittle.

The author and his granddaughter Charlotte walking in the Cuillin near Glenbrittle.

Glenbrittle beach on Boxing Day 2008.

'Sea Flower' seaweed on the beach.

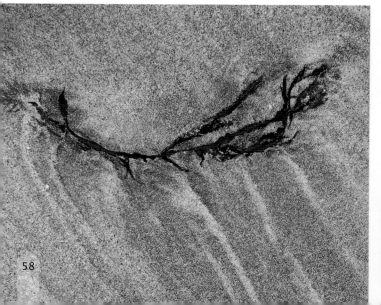

Glenbrittle beach on May Bank Holiday 2009.

Moon over the Cuillin.

The view from the beach
at Glenbrittle.

This old church above Carbost has been sympathetically converted into a residential dwelling.

The waterfall at Carbost. After even moderate rainfall this waterfall becomes a raging torrent as water from the surrounding hills drains into Loch Harport.

Ewe with new lamb.

The Old Schoolhouse above Carbost. At one time the children from Carbost village had a long, steep climb to school every morning.

Skye and Floss in their natural surroundings.

Talisker Distillery lies on the shores of Loch Harport and is Skye's one and only distillery.

Sunset over
Loch Harport.

The May on Loch Harport.

Herons are common and can readily be seen patiently waiting for prey to come within range.

Unwary sheep stranded at Drynoch.

Loch Harport in summer and winter.

Talisker Bay at dawn.

George and Oddy, friends and walking companions, near Laimhrig na Moine. To the north is Talisker Bay.

Yellow Iris grow wild in great profusion during summer.

Cattle often roam the lesser-used roads.

A crofter moves his sheep using two of his most valuable tools: his dog and his quad bike.

Common Buzzard feeding on a Red Deer head.

Bog Cotton grows on the moorland in early spring. Here a single bloom is caught in the evening sunlight.

Rocks above Glen Eynort.

An anchor and creel buoys being used as garden ornaments.

The Cuillin ridge from the top of Glen Eynort.

An old byre near
Portnalong.

Highland cow in Glenbrittle.

Detail from a long-abandoned crofthouse.

Meadows, such as this one at
Drynoch, are a profusion of
wild flowers in the late spring.

A Red Stag seen outside the
author's house.

Sunlight streams through conifer trees in Glenvarragill.

The Isle of Skye Pipe Band often gives displays on summer evenings in Somerled Square, Portree.

The forest to the south of Portree has many miles of beautiful walking paths.

Rowan trees grow in large numbers all over Skye. An abundant crop of berries could indicate a hard winter to come.

Foxgloves growing wild by the roadside between Sligachan and Portree.

75

The 'boys' from the fish farm go out across the bay to tend to their salmon crop.

One of the local trawlermen.

A view of Portree harbour from out in the bay.

Summer brings the watersports enthusiasts out. Warm summer days will often see one or two jet skis in Portree Bay.

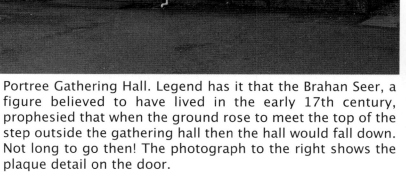

Portree Gathering Hall. Legend has it that the Brahan Seer, a figure believed to have lived in the early 17th century, prophesied that when the ground rose to meet the top of the step outside the gathering hall then the hall would fall down. Not long to go then! The photograph to the right shows the plaque detail on the door.

The Apothecary's Tower stands on top of the Meall, a wooded peninsula known locally as the 'Lump'. The tower served as sign to passing ships that medical supplies and expertise were available in Portree.

The 'Lump' also plays host to Skye's annual Highland Games, which take place in a natural amphitheatre overlooking Portree.

Fishing boat with obligatory seagulls, Portree.

BRD 632

The *Deutschland* attracts 'boys' of all ages and sizes!

The *Hebridean Princess* (above) and the *Saga Ruby* (below) are just two of the cruise liners that regularly visit Portree.

The RNLB Lifeboat based in Portree is the *Stanley Watson Barker* and performs valuable local service.

White-tailed sea eagle.

The beach at Camas Ban.

A view of the harbour from the top of the Apothecary's Tower.

North-East Skye

Loch Fada.

Digging peats. High fuel prices have seen a number of people returning to this form of heating in recent times.

Fishing for trout on the Storr Lochs.

The early morning sun lights up
the Storr in midwinter.

The Old Man of Storr.

A rock stack near Lealt Falls.

Autumn gold.

The view south from Inver Tote.

Part of the old diatomite workings at Inver Tote. This building used to house a furnace, storage and drying facilities.

This sign at Kilt Rock indicates the Jurrasic history of the Trotternish Peninsula.

Kilt Rock and its famous waterfall.

Kilt Rock seen from Brothers' Point.

Two heart-shaped pebbles on the shore at Brothers' Point.

Looking south from Kilt Rock.

Part of the Trotternish Ridge near Staffin.

The Quirang. Photographers are to be found in abundance here nearly all year round as they try to catch the dawn and sunrise lighting up parts of the Trotternish Ridge.

Dawn light begins to illuminate the Cleat and its adjoining loch.

The road up to the Quirang car park is steep and twisting.

Glaspein and part of the Quirang beyond.

Tulm Island, Duntulm Bay.

Gorse and wild primroses flourish anywhere they can establish a foothold.

Former coastguard cottages at Duntulm.

Flora MacDonald's grave at Kilmuir.

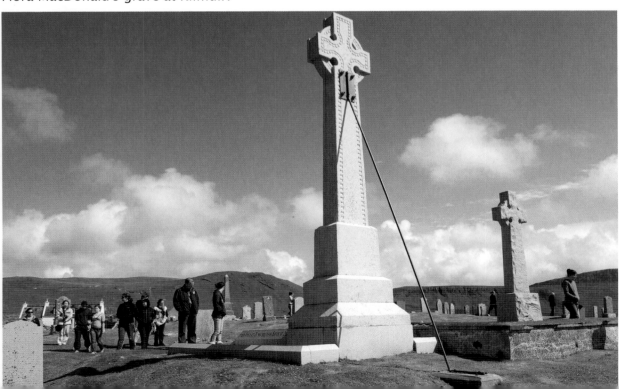

The Museum of Skye Life.

Sunset at Uig looking towards Waternish.

Even on the exposed northern coast of Skye gardens can flourish.

Calmac ferry arrives at Uig from the Western Isles.

Fairy Glen near Sheader Uig. This unique and strange landscape is believed to have been created by small landslides which were then further sculpted by glaciation.

A Rowan tree wards off evil spirits in the Fairy Glen.

Fraser's Folly, Uig, built in the 1890s by Captain Fraser, the Laird of the day. This castle-like structure could have been used as a place where the tenants paid their rents.

North-West Skye

Gesto Farm with Loch Harport and the Cuillin beyond.

Pictish stone at Tote.

Farmland at Skeabost.

A croft building near Harlosh.

Wray Island from Ullinish.

Cuillin from Drynoch.

Lichen on Dun Beag Broch near Struan.

Fire Brigade hut at Struan (no longer there).

Portnalong from Gesto.

Wind turbines seen from near Dunvegan.

Dunvegan Post Office.

Loch Bracadale from Gesto.

MacLeod's Tables from near Roskhill.

Ardtrek Point, where Loch Harport and Loch Bracadale converge.

Loch Beag from Struan.

Dunvegan Castle
from Uiginish.

Part of Dunvegan village from Uiginish.

Judging sheep at Dunvegan Show, 2008.

A water lily in Dunvegan Castle grounds.

Dunvegan Castle grounds.

Coral beach, which is not made from coral but millions upon millions of seashells.

119

Hooded crow with bread.

Lapwing in a wildflower meadow.

Great skua.

Red boat, Stein.

Stein Inn at Stein, Waternish, where a visitor enjoys a pint on a hot day in August.

Fuchsia at Stein.

Sheep grazing
at Waterstein.

Wheatear.

Glendale and Loch Pooltiel.

Coming home. Dusk at Waternish.

Moonen Bay.

Ruined church and cemetery at Trumpan.

Neist Point.

Waves driven by
gale force winds at
Neist Point.

Neist Point lighthouse.

Oystercatcher.

Gannet.

Cairn field, Neist Point.